EMOJIPEDIA

WELDONOWEN
PUBLISHING

WELDON OWEN
PUBLISHING

A division of Bonnier Publishing
King's Road Publishing
2.07 The Plaza, 535 Kings Road
Chelsea, London, SW10 0SZ

Created by:
Illustrator: Bernard Chau
Design: Gareth Butterworth and Tania Gomes
Managing editor: Hazel Eriksson
Publisher: Donna Gregory

Copyright 2016 by Weldon Owen Ltd.

All rights reserved. No part of this publication may be reproduced, stored in a retrieval system
or transmitted in any form or by any means, electronic, mechanical, photocopying, recording,
or otherwise, without the permission of the copyright holder and the publisher.

Printed in the EU

10 9 8 7 6 5 4 3

ISBN 978-1-78342-258-6

weldonowen.co.uk

bonnierpublishing.com

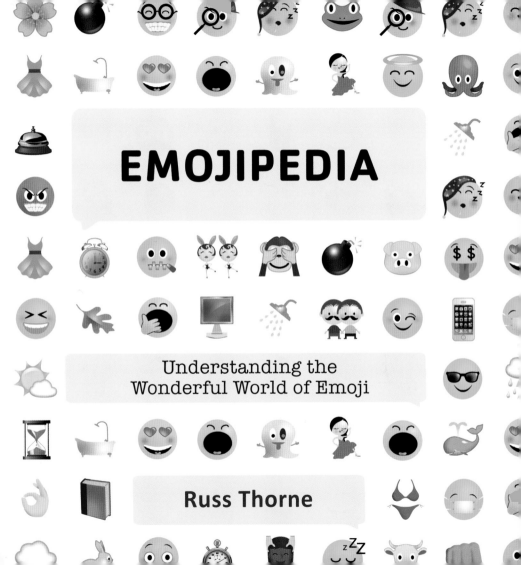

EMOJIPEDIA

Understanding the
Wonderful World of Emoji

Russ Thorne

CONTENTS

INTRODUCING EMOJI

Emoji: from the Japanese (e = picture) + (moji = written character)

The little smiling faces we can drop into messages have become an integral part of the way we communicate. So much so, in fact, that the *Oxford English Dictionary* named the "Face with tears of joy" emoji its word of the year for 2015 – evidence of the key part emoji increasingly play in our daily interactions.

In the Beginning

Like so many things in the modern world – Twitter®, Instagram®, Taylor Swift – emoji feel like they've always been around. But they're actually relatively recent arrivals on the global scene. They only really entered mass popular culture in the West around 2010 (two years after "Love Story", Taylor fans), and even then didn't gain huge popularity until 2011, when Apple® added an emoji keyboard to the iPhone® operating system. Before then, emoji (there's debate over whether the plural

The Japanese origin of emoji can still be felt in many of the traditional images, like the bamboo good luck charm shown above.

is emoji or emojis; we've used emoji, which is the Japanese way) were pretty much an exclusively Japanese phenomenon. The earliest Japanese emoji – crude, 12-pixel graphics – appeared on telephone handsets in 1997, but became much more widely available in 1999 on pagers and mobile phones used by teenagers.

These early emoji were embraced by young Japanese women, who found the little symbols *kawaii* – a concept that roughly translates as "cute". Their use spread organically, until they were a ubiquitous part of electronic communication in the country – so much so that the iPhone® didn't take off in Japan at first, as it didn't support emoji.

How did emoji go from cute niche art to global megastars (there's Taylor Swift again)? Enter the Unicode Consortium, who sound like James

Bond villains but are actually an international software industry body whose members include Apple®, Google®, Samsung®, and Microsoft®, among others. They created a standardized emoji set in 2010, which formed the basis for all the emoji we currently use.

Same Face, Many Masks

The unified emoji set meant that all emoji have the same code and name, regardless of the device or software platform you use them on. So when you select "Face with tears of joy", you're picking the same emoji whether you're on an iPhone®, Android®, or a Windows® tablet.

However, while the name stays the same, the exact appearance doesn't. Each platform designs the way their emoji look, giving them a distinctive personality depending on the device you use. It's like giving a book different covers: the story inside stays the same, but the packaging looks a little different. Take a look at the box (right) for some examples.

So What Does it Mean?

So are emoji supposed to symbolize the one specific thing their name suggests? Not quite. The name is just a description to distinguish one symbol from

VARIATIONS

Some variations are more significant than others – just look how these emoji differ across the platforms!

Apple®	Android®	Samsung®

Apple®	Android®	Samsung®

Apple®	Samsung®

Apple®	Google 1®

Apple®	Android®

another. Some names are obviously reflective of the emoji itself – "Smiling face with smiling eyes", for example, has a pretty clear meaning, while others are more ambiguous; "Tired face" could just as easily be cranky or freaked out. So users will have to hope the context clarifies the meaning. (And as for just what the "Smiling cat face with heart-shaped eyes" is supposed to mean, well, life is full of mysteries...)

Smiling face
with smiling
eyes

Tired face

Smiling cat face
with heart-
shaped eyes

All of this ambiguity about names and usage means that there's no one way we're "supposed" to use emoji, even if their creators may have had a use in mind for each symbol. Their use and interpretation depends on us, and the way we communicate, just as speech (and slang use) does; and can also vary between countries and cultures, and change over time.

A New Language?

There's even discussion about whether or not emoji

LOST IN TRANSLATION

The above emoji phrase translates to "bombshell" in English, meaning a stunning person or a shocking action. ("She really dropped a bombshell.") But this same combination of emoji may be completely meaningless to a Swedish or Hindi speaker.

could be considered a language of their own. With their wide range of symbols and icons that express everything from emotional state and food cravings to work and travel plans, are they a kind of twenty-first century pop art hieroglyphics?

The Unicode Consortium think not. Their official website argues that emoji lack the grammar and vocabulary to really be a language, and that the symbols aren't totally universal. Emoji phrases that play on words might work between speakers of the same language, but would be incomprehensible to someone from another culture, where the phrase doesn't exist and the symbols don't carry the same meanings (see box, above).

On the other hand, there are certainly some "language-like" qualities to emoji: in particular, they can help us add tone of voice and other subtleties, something that can often be lacking in our emails, tweets, and messages. What could be more language-like than enabling clear communication of our real meaning? Sometimes adding a heart or an expressive emoji can make all the difference.

The Good, the Bad, the Taco

Emoji can indeed empower us, but as people aren't perfect, neither are emoji – a deceitful one can help us lie about standing friends up, for example, or dismiss bad behaviour with a throwaway winky face.

But the emoji story isn't complete – new symbols arrive, new etiquette (emojiquette?) evolves, we twist and mould them to our needs, as we do with all forms of communication.

And the library is constantly growing. Online petitions for the addition of cheese and taco emoji led to both symbols being included, and rumours abound that bacon, avocados, and even Mrs Claus are in development. Who knows what could be next?

The Human Touch

All of which goes to show that people are increasingly taking emoji to heart. They can be used in all manner of situations: work, play, art, love, etc. (There are even plenty of alternative, more risqué interpretations of seemingly innocent emoji, for when we're feeling frisky!)

Equally, they can help us sympathize, argue, support others, break up, get together, or even plan what's for dinner tonight. We can write poetry with emoji or just blow a kiss to our partners. Emoji may have started small, but now they're helping millions of people communicate and are keeping our human interactions just that: human, with all our quirks and oddities. And that's got be worth a "Grinning face with smiling eyes"!

Now go forth and send some emoji!

THE EMOJI

The following pages contain every current emoji, with their official names. Commonly assumed meanings are in italics where they differ from the emoji's primary definition.

The emoji are organized as per Apple's® keyboard, but check the index on page 122 if you're having any trouble finding what you want.

SMILEYS & PEOPLE

Grinning face

Grimacing face

Grinning face with
smiling eyes
Cringe, wince, or *chilly*

Face with tears of joy

Smiling face with
open mouth

Smiling face with open
mouth and smiling eyes

Smiling face with open
mouth and cold sweat

Smiling face with open
mouth and
tightly-closed eyes

Smiling face with halo

Winking face

Smiling face with
smiling eyes
Best friend

Slightly smiling face

Upside-down face
Foolishness or *tipsy*

White smiling face

Face savouring
delicious food
Silly

Relieved face
Calm or *content*

Smiling face with
heart-shaped eyes
Love of a person or *thing*

Face throwing a kiss

Kissing face

WHITE EMOJI

The "white" smiling
and frowning faces
predate modern
emoji, appearing
as above in earlier
incarnations.

"White" in this
context is a relic of
pre-emoji unicode
language, referring
not to ethnicity
but to a hollow
character drawn as
an outline.

Kissing face with
smiling eyes

Kissing face with
closed eyes
Intimacy

Face with stuck-out
tongue and winking eye
Kookiness

Face with stuck-out
tongue and
tightly closed eyes

Face with stuck-out
tongue

Money-mouth face
Dollar!

Nerd face

Smiling face
with sunglasses
Cool

Hugging face

Smirking face

Face without mouth

Neutral face

Expressionless face

Unamused face

Face with rolling eyes

Thinking face

Flushed face
Embarrassed

Disappointed face
Sad

Worried face

Angry face

Pouting face

Pensive face
Remorseful or *sorrowful*

Confused face

Slightly frowning face

White frowning face

Persevering face
Helplessness

Confounded face
Freaking out

Tired face

Weary face

Face with look of triumph
Frustration, annoyance

Face with open mouth
Surprise or *oral sex,
if repeated*

Face screaming in fear
Melodramatic shock

Fearful face

Face with open mouth
and cold sweat

Hushed face

Frowning face with
open mouth

Anguished face

Crying face

Disappointed but
relieved face

Sleepy face

Face with cold sweat

Loudly crying face

Dizzy face

Astonished face

Zipper-mouth face
Lips are sealed

Face with medical mask
Illness or a bad smell

Face with thermometer
Illness

Face with head bandage
Injury

Sleeping face

SLEEPY FACE

Emoji with a droplet or droplets are not always what we might assume. This face is "sleepy", not "crying". In this case, the droplet is sleep-drool or a snot bubble, a visual cue borrowed from Japanese manga and anime. Luckily there are other options to indicate sleep without suggesting you might drool!

Sleeping symbol
Bored

Pile of poo

Smiling face with horns
Mischief or *wickedness*

Imp

THE POO EMOJI

One of the oldest and most beloved emoji, this symbol was part of the original Japanese sets (where it was very popular), and has cultural roots in 1980s cartoons like Dr. Slump, where a similar-looking character was an object of fun.

In its current form it can naturally be offensive, but it's also a gentle, even sympathetic way of acknowledging that a situation is, quite frankly, a bit shit. It's a far more eloquent "dislike" than a simple thumbs down and symbolizes the true purpose of emoji: adding a little more human emotion to our written communication.

Japanese ogre

Japanese goblin

Skull
Death or *danger*

A ghost!

Extraterrestrial alien

Robot face

Smiling cat face with open mouth

Grinning cat face with smiling eyes

Cat face with tears of joy

Smiling cat face with heart-shaped eyes

Cat face with wry smile

Kissing cat face with closed eyes

Weary cat face

Crying cat face

Pouting cat face

Person raising both hands in celebration

Clapping hands sign

Waving hand sign

Thumbs up sign

Thumbs down sign

Fisted hand sign
Punch or fist bump

Raised fist
*A salute or a reference
to masturbation*

Victory hand
Peace

OK hand sign

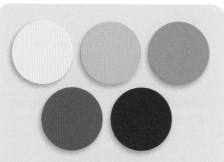

MODIFIERS

Many of the faces and hands in this section
support skin tone "modifiers", which allow
the emoji to reflect the diversity of human
skin tones.

A pop-up menu within the emoji keyboard
offers five alternatives to yellow, based on
the Fitzpatrick Scale – a dermatological tool
used to classify skin types.

Raised hand
Stop or *high-five*

Open hands sign
Hug or *jazz hands*

Flexed biceps

Person with folded hands
Apologies, a prayer, or
a *high-five*

Up pointing index
Secret or *question*

Up pointing
backhand index

Down pointing
backhand index

Left (or right) pointing
backhand index

Reversed hand with
middle finger extended
Insult

Raised hand with
fingers splayed
Waving or *five*

Sign of the horns
Heavy metal or *rock*

Vulcan salute
Live long and prosper

Writing hand

Nail polish
Nonchalance

Mouth
Talking

Tongue
Silliness or *a taunt*
Oral sex, if repeated

Ear
Listening

Nose
Smelling

Eye
Looking or *watching*

Eyes
Looking or *watching*

Bust in silhouette

Busts in silhouette

Speaking head in silhouette

Baby

Boy

Girl

Man

Woman

Person with blond hair

Older man

Older woman

Man with Gua Pi Mao
(a type of Chinese hat)

Man with turban

Police officer

Construction worker

Guardsman

Sleuth or spy

Father Christmas

Baby angel

Princess

COUPLES

Whether holding hands, feeling the love, or sharing a smooch, users can select two men, two women, or a woman and a man. The range of "family" emoji similarly offers various options, giving users greater likelihood of finding symbols representative of their own families.

Bride with veil

Pedestrian
Walking

Runner
Running or
"Get out of there!"

Dancer
Party time!

Woman with bunny ears
Going out with friends

Couple holding hands
(multiple variations
exist)

Person bowing deeply
Humility

Information desk person
Sarcasm

Face with "no good"
gesture

Face with OK gesture

Happy person raising
one hand
Hello or *"I know!"*

Person frowning

Person with pouting face

Haircut

Face massage

Couple with heart

Kiss

Family
(multiple variations
exist)

25

Woman's clothes

T-shirt

Jeans

Necktie

Dress

Bikini

Kimono

Lipstick

Kiss mark

Footprints

High-heeled shoe

Woman's sandal

Woman's boot

Man's shoe

Athletic shoe

Woman's hat

Top hat

Graduation cap

Crown

Hard hat

EMOJI IN SNAPCHAT®

In November 2015, Kylie Jenner followed in her big sister Kim Kardashian's footsteps and "broke" the Internet when a crown symbol appeared on her Snapchat® profile.

Snapchat® uses only limited emoji, and these have very specific meanings, which have to be earned through use of the app. For example, "Baby" denotes a new friend, "Smiling face with smiling eyes" a best friend, and the coveted "Golden heart" a number one best friend. The crown is unique to Kylie, and cannot be used by anyone else – and as Snapchat's® most followed person, she deserves it!

School satchel

Pouch

Purse

Handbag

Briefcase

Eyeglasses

Dark sunglasses

Ring

Closed umbrella

ANIMALS & NATURE

Dog face

Cat face

Mouse face

Hamster face

Rabbit face

Bear face

Panda face

Koala

Tiger face

Lion face

Cow face

Pig face

29

Pig nose

Frog face

Octopus

Monkey face

MONKEY BUSINESS

The "Hear-no- / See-no- / Speak-no-evil" monkeys are useful in all kinds of situations. They can suggest that you don't know anything about a subject or situation, that you do and that you're keeping it secret, or that you're trying to unsee / unspeak / unhear something. Or maybe you're just at the zoo!

See-no-evil monkey

Hear-no-evil monkey

Speak-no-evil monkey

Monkey

Chicken

Penguin

Bird

Baby chick

Hatching chick

Front-facing baby chick

Wolf face

Boar

Horse face

Unicorn face

Honeybee

Bug

Snail

Ladybird

Ant

Spider

Scorpion

Crab
Crabby

Snake

Turtle

Tropical fish

Fish

Blowfish
*"Fugu", a delicacy
in Japan,* or *bloated*

Dolphin

Spouting whale

Whale

Crocodile

Leopard

Tiger

Water buffalo

Ox

ONE HUMP OR TWO?

It has been a source of heated discussion online why the Unicode Consortium thought two types of camel necessary, but didn't include cheese until 2015.

The camel's most notorious use is to instigate humping, and with two options to choose from, users can specify just how many humps they want to convey!

Cow

Dromedary camel
Hump day!
Wanna hump?

Bactrian camel
Double the humping power!

Elephant

Goat

Ram

Sheep

Horse

Pig

Rat

Mouse

Rooster
Wake up!

Turkey
Thanksgiving

Dove of peace
Peace, conflict resolution

Dog

Poodle

Cat

Rabbit

Chipmunk

Paw prints

Dragon

Dragon face

Cactus

Christmas tree

Evergreen tree

Deciduous tree

Palm tree

Seedling

Herb

Shamrock

Four leaf clover
Lucky

BIG IN JAPAN

Emoji's Japanese origin is clearly visible in symbols like the Kadomatsu, which is a New Year's decoration made of bamboo or pine. It is meant to bring good luck.

The weighting of food and drink symbols toward Japanese dishes, such as rice, sushi, and the green tea served in sushi restaurants, as well as bento boxes and oden, also shows the Japanese origins of emoji. More recent additions, like the taco, illustrate their increasingly global nature.

Kadomatsu (Japanese
New Year's decoration)

Tanabata tree
(Japanese wish tree)

Leaf fluttering in wind

Fallen leaf
Autumn

Maple leaf

Ear of rice

Hibiscus

Sunflower

Rose

Tulip

Blossom

Cherry blossom

Bouquet

Mushroom

Chestnut

Jack-o-lantern
Halloween

Spiral shell

Spiderweb

Earth
(various views exist)

Full moon symbol

Waning gibbous
moon symbol (flip for
waxing gibbous)

Last quarter
moon symbol (flip for
first quarter moon)

Waning crescent moon
symbol (flip for waxing
crescent moon)

New moon symbol

New moon with face

Full moon with face

First quarter moon
with face (flip for last
quarter moon with face)

Sun with face

Crescent moon

White medium star

Glowing star

Dizzy symbol

Sparkles

Comet

Black sun with rays

BLACK EMOJI

Like the "white" emoji mentioned on page 13, "black" does not refer to colour, but to the original unicode used to create this image. The first iteration of "Black sun with rays" was a solid image, as seen above.

White sun with small cloud

Sun behind cloud

White sun behind cloud

ANIMALS & NATURE

White sun behind cloud
with rain

Cloud

Cloud with rain

Thunder cloud and rain

Cloud with lightning

High-voltage sign

Fire
Burn!

Collision symbol

Snowflake

Cloud with snow

Snowman

Snowman without snow

Wind blowing face

Dash symbol
*Pair with another emoji
to show speed*

Cloud with tornado

Fog
Grumpiness

Umbrella

Umbrella with rain drops

Droplet

WET AND WILD

The splashing
sweat symbol is
another symbol
borrowed from
Japanese comics,
where it indicates
effort or exertion.
It is also commonly
used to show
splashing water or
rain, or if you're
feeling intimate,
it can also suggest
various other fluids
(we'll leave that to
your imagination).

Splashing sweat symbol

Water wave

FOOD & DRINK

Green apple

Red apple

Pear

Tangerine

Lemon

Banana

Watermelon

Grapes

Strawberry

Melon

Cherries

Peach
*Bottom, breasts, or even
female genitalia*

Pineapple

Tomato

Aubergine
Male genitalia

Hot pepper
Hot stuff!

Ear of maize

Roasted sweet potato

Honey pot

Bread

Cheese wedge

Poultry leg

Meat on bone

Fried shrimp

Cooking (or fried egg)

Hamburger

French fries

Hot dog
Male genitalia

LOOK CLOSELY

If you look closely at "French fries" you will see that this emoji is branded with another emoji!

It looks like "Smiling face with smiling eyes" – someone on the design team must have been excited about fries!

Slice of pizza

Spaghetti

Taco
Female genitalia

Burrito

Steaming bowl

Pot of food

Fishcake with swirl design

Sushi

Bento box

Curry and rice

Rice ball

Cooked rice

Rice cracker

Oden (a kind of Japanese kebab)

Dango
Dessert on a stick

Shaved ice

Ice cream

Soft ice cream

Shortcake

Birthday cake

Custard

Candy
Sweet

Lollipop

Chocolate bar

Popcorn

Doughnut
Combine with a pointing finger for sexy times

Cookie

Beer mug

Clinking beer mugs
Cheers!

Wine glass

Cocktail glass

Tropical drink
Vacation

Bottle with popping cork
Celebration

Sake bottle and cup

Teacup without handle

Hot beverage

Baby bottle

Fork and knife

Fork and knife with plate

ACTIVITIES

Football

Basketball and hoop

American football

Baseball

CUE THE MAGIC

Billiards (or pool) appears very differently across mobile platforms. Some opt for the various coloured balls of the game, while others use the black eight ball. The latter has a similarity to the "Magic 8 Ball" toy, giving Apple® keyboard users an alternative use if they would like to suggest uncertainty or maybe the need to consult a mystic power.

Similarly, Apple® only show the balls of all the sports on this page, while other platforms include rackets and hoops.

Tennis racquet and ball

Volleyball

Rugby ball

Billiards
Who knows – consult the Magic 8 Ball

Flag in hole

Golfer

Table tennis paddle
and ball

Badminton racket
and shuttlecock

Ice hockey stick
and puck

Field hockey stick
and ball

Cricket bat and ball

Ski and ski boot

Skier

Snowboarder

Ice skate

Bow and arrow

Fishing pole and fish

Rowboat

Swimmer

Surfer

Bath

Person with ball

Weight lifter

Bicyclist

Mountain bicyclist

Horse racing

Man in business suit
levitating

Trophy

Running shirt with sash

Sports medal

Military medal

Reminder ribbon

Rosette

Ticket

Admission tickets

Performing arts

JUMP!

Yes, that icon is a businessman levitating. Apparently he's meant to be an anthropomorphized exclamation mark. It's a marvel human civilization made it this far without him!

His name is Walt Jabsco, by the way, in homage to the artwork of Ska pioneers The Specials and Two Tone records.

Artist palette

Circus tent

Microphone

Headphone

Musical score

Musical keyboard

Saxophone

Trumpet

Guitar

Violin

Clapperboard
Cut!

Video game

Alien monster

Direct hit

Game die
Do you feel lucky?

Slot machine
Jackpot!

Bowling

TRAVEL & PLACES

Automobile
Driving or *travelling*

Taxi

Recreational vehicle

Bus

Trolleybus

Racing car

Police car

Ambulance
Emergency!

Fire engine

Minibus

Delivery truck

Articulated lorry

Tractor

Racing motorcycle

Bicycle

Police car's
revolving light
Crisis!

Oncoming police car

Oncoming bus

Oncoming automobile

Oncoming taxi

Aerial tramway

Mountain cableway

Suspension railway

Railway car

Tram car

Monorail

High-speed train

High-speed train with bullet nose

HOPPING A TRAIN

The "High-speed train with bullet nose" emoji is modelled on the original Shinkansen – the Japanese bullet train.

Japan was the first country to build dedicated railway lines for high-speed travel. In fact, the term "bullet train" is a literal translation of the Japanese term *dangan ressha*, a nickname given to the Shinkansen project while it was initially being discussed in the 1930s. The name stuck because of the original 0 Series Shinkansen's resemblance to a bullet and its high speed.

Light rail

Mountain railway

Steam locomotive

Train

Metro
Tunnel of love

Tram

Station

Helicopter

Small airplane

Airplane

Airplane departure

Airplane arriving

Sailboat

Motorboat

Speedboat

Ferry

Passenger ship

Rocket
Sky rockets in flight...

Satellite

Seat

Anchor

Construction sign
Caution!

Fuel pump

Bus stop

Vertical traffic light

Horizontal traffic light

Chequered flag
Go!

Ship

Ferris wheel

Roller coaster

Carousel horse

Building construction

Foggy

Tokyo Tower

Factory

Fountain

Moon viewing
ceremony

Mountain

MOON VIEWING CEREMONY

The moon viewing ceremony is a part of the Japanese Mid-Autumn festival. Traditions include displaying decorations made from Japanese Pampas grass and eating rice dumplings in order to celebrate the beauty of the moon.

Snowcapped mountain

Mount Fuji

Volcano
A particularly explosive encounter

Silhouette of Japan

Camping

Tent

National park

Motorway

Railway track

Sunrise

Sunrise over mountains

Desert

Beach with umbrella

Desert island

Sunset over buildings

Cityscape at dusk

Cityscape

Night with stars

Bridge at night

Milky Way

Shooting star

Firework sparkler

Fireworks

Rainbow
LGBT pride

House buildings

European castle

Japanese castle

Stadium

Statue of Liberty

House building

House with garden

Derelict house building

Office building

Department store

Japanese post office

European post office

Hospital

Bank

Hotel

Convenience store

School

Love hotel
A liaison

Wedding

Classical building

SUMMING IT UP

Emoji institutions are represented in nearly every platform with generic buildings that have small clues as to their purpose, as seen on these pages. The Microsoft® emoji keyboard alone deviates from this strategy, instead showing simple graphics representing the buildings' functions. The "School" emoji shows an apple, a ruler, and a pencil (seen above), the "Bank" shows a coinbank icon, the "Hotel" a bed, and so on. These versions are more versatile to use, but less readily identifiable.

Church

Mosque

Synagogue

Kaaba

FAITHFUL REPRESENTATIONS

Emoji can be used to communicate faith with symbols of churches, mosques, and synagogues for Christianity, Islam, and Judaism respectively. There's also the Kaaba ("the cube"), the building at the centre of Islam's holiest site, the Al-Masjid al-Haram mosque in Mecca; and a Shinto shrine, referring to the diverse Japanese religion that emphasizes ritual practices at shrines and making supplications to the kami – a host of gods or spirits.

A Buddha emoji was on the original inclusion list for Unicode 8.0, but was removed due to Unicode selection criteria, which advises against adding emoji of people or deities.

Shinto shrine

OBJECTS

Watch

Mobile phone

Mobile phone with
rightwards arrow at left

Personal computer

Keyboard

Desktop computer

Printer

Mouse

Trackball

Joystick

Compression

Minidisc

Floppy disk

Optical disc

DVD

Videocassette

OUT OF TIME

Some of the objects on this page – faxes, floppy disks, and pagers – seem slightly old-fashioned now. They're relics of the first emoji, which came from a much more analogue age, but still have their uses, especially if you're planning an eighties party.

Camera

Camera with flash

Video camera

Movie camera

Film projector

Film frames

Telephone receiver

Black telephone

Pager

Fax machine

Television

Radio

Studio microphone

Level slider

Control knobs

Stopwatch

Timer clock

Alarm clock

Mantelpiece clock

Hourglass with flowing sand

Hourglass

Satellite antenna

Battery

Electric plug

Electric lightbulb

Torch

Candle

Wastebasket

Oil drum

Money with wings

Banknote with dollar sign

Banknote with yen sign

Banknote with euro sign

Banknote with pound sign

Money bag

Credit card

Gem stone

Scales

Wrench

Hammer

Hammer and pick

Hammer and wrench

Pick

Nut and bolt

Gear

Chain

Pistol

Bomb

Hocho
(Japanese cooking knife)

Dagger knife

Crossed swords

Shield

Smoking symbol

Skull and crossbones
Poison or *Pirates!*

Coffin

Funeral urn

Amphora (an ancient style of ceramic vase)

Crystal ball

Prayer beads

Barber pole

Alembic
(for distillation)

Telescope

OBJECTS OF AMUSEMENT

Emoji aren't without a sense of humour. It may be no coincidence that the smoking symbol is immediately followed by the skull and crossbones and a coffin in the Apple® keyboard layout. For example, the bomb symbol could be seen as violent, but comes across as more lighthearted – it's used to describe a powerful song, a dramatic development, or to imply that the fuse has been lit and a situation is going to explode. Elsewhere, we've probably all felt that our money has left us so quickly that it must have wings.

Microscope

Hole

Pill

Syringe

THE HOLE PICTURE

The hole emoji is a versatile one. It's used for suggesting hunger ("my stomach is like a..."), a general sense of emptiness ("I feel so..."), the idea that a place is capable of swallowing up anything ("my room =..."), and a sense of embarrassment so acute that you want to crawl into a hole and vanish ("it was so awkward I just..."). Astrophysics fans can also use it as a black hole.

Thermometer

Label

Bookmark

Toilet

Shower

Bathtub

Key

Old key

Couch and lamp

Sleeping accommodation

Bed

Door

Bellhop bell

Frame with picture

World map

Umbrella on ground

Moyai

Shopping bags

OBJECTS

Balloon

Carp streamer
(a decoration for Japan's
Children's Day)

Ribbon

Wrapped present

Confetti ball

Party popper

WHAT'S HE DOING HERE?

Japanese culture is understandably the driving force behind many emoji, which explains some potentially confusing inclusions. The "Moyai", for example, is a reference to the famous Easter Island statues, but also a statue near Shibuya station in Tokyo. The same goes for the "Carp streamer", which is a popular sight on Children's Day in Japan. The world is still waiting for a Godzilla emoji.

Japanese dolls

Wind chime

Crossed flags

Izakaya lantern
(Traditionally hung
outside pubs in Japan)

Envelope

Envelope with
downwards arrow above

Incoming envelope

E-mail symbol

Love letter

Postbox

Closed mailbox with
lowered flag

Closed mailbox with
raised flag

Open mailbox with
raised flag

Open mailbox with
lowered flag

Package

Postal horn

Inbox tray

Outbox tray

Scroll

Page with curl

Bookmark tabs

Bar chart

Chart with upwards trend

Chart with downwards trend

Page facing up

Calendar

Spiral calendar pad

Card index

Card file box

Ballot box with ballot

File cabinet

Clipboard

Spiral notepad

File folder

Open file folder

Card index dividers

Rolled-up newspaper

Newspaper

Notebook

Closed book
(other colours available)

Notebook with
decorative cover

Ledger

TAKING A PAGE FROM APPLE®

In the Apple® version of the "Open book" emoji, the text is legible if you magnify it, and is an excerpt from an Apple® advertising campaign from the late 90s:

Here's to the crazy ones. The misfits. The rebels. The troublemakers. The round pegs in the square holes.

The ones who see things differently. They're not fond of rules. And they have no respect for the status quo. You can quote them, disagree with them, glorify or vilify them.

About the only thing you can't do is...

Books

Open book

Link symbol

Paperclip

Linked paperclips

Black scissors

Triangular ruler

Straight ruler

Pushpin

Round pushpin

Triangular flag on post

Waving white flag
Surrender

Waving black flag
Cancel or disqualify

Closed lock with key

Lock

Open lock

Lock with ink pen

Lower left ballpoint pen

Lower left fountain pen

Black nib

Memo

Pencil

Lower left crayon

Lower left paintbrush

Magnifying glass
(can point left or right)

SYMBOLS

Heavy black heart
(other colours available)

Broken heart

Heavy heart exclamation
mark ornament

Two hearts

Revolving hearts

Beating heart

HEAVY HEARTS

Why the heavy black heart? It refers to the original description of the emoji, as a solid black shape displayed on a monochrome screen. The name has remained, even though there are many different colours to choose from now.

Other heart symbols add depth to your declaration of love: "Revolving hearts" suggests a giddy, excited love, and "Heart with ribbon" is about giving your gift-wrapped heart away, like a present. Let's hope it doesn't end with "Broken heart".

Growing heart

Sparkling heart

SYMBOLS

Heart with arrow

Heart with ribbon

Heart decoration

Peace symbol

Latin cross

Star and crescent

Om symbol

Wheel of dharma

Star of David

Six-pointed star with middle dot

Menorah with nine branches

Yin and yang

Orthodox cross

Place of worship

Ophiuchus (potential 13th sign of the zodiac)

Aries

Taurus

Gemini

Cancer
69

Leo

Virgo

Libra

Scorpius

Sagittarius

Capricorn

Aquarius

Pisces

Squared ID

Atom symbol

Squared cjk unified
ideograph 7a7a
Available or *vacant*

Squared cjk unified
ideograph 5272
Sale or *bargain*

Radioactive sign

Biohazard sign

Mobile phone off

Vibration mode

Squared cjk unified
ideograph 6709
Own or *possess*

Squared cjk unified
ideograph 7121
Lack

Squared cjk unified
ideograph 7533
Request or *monkey*

Squared cjk unified
ideograph 55b6
Work or *open for business*

Squared cjk unified
ideograph 6708
Moon or *month*

Eight-pointed black star

Squared VS

Circled ideograph
Accept

White flower

Circled ideograph
Advantage

Circled ideograph
Secret

Circled ideograph
Congratulations

Squared cjk unified
ideograph 5408
Agree or *unite*

Squared cjk unified
ideograph 6e80
Full

Squared cjk unified
ideograph 7981
Forbidden

Negative squared latin
capital letter A
Blood type A

Negative squared latin
capital letter B
Blood type B

Negative squared AB
Blood type AB

Squared CL
Clear

Negative squared latin
capital letter O
Blood type O

Squared SOS

No entry

Name badge

No entry sign

Cross mark

Heavy large circle

Anger symbol

Hot springs

No pedestrians

Do not litter symbol

No bicycles

Non-potable water symbol

ANGER MANAGEMENT

The "Anger symbol" emoji comes from Manga and anime. It indicates the rage lines around a character's face as they get increasingly furious; it could also hint at the onomatopoeic "zap!" and "pow!" sound effect bubbles in comics.

No one under eighteen symbol

No mobile phones

Heavy exclamation mark symbol (white version also available)

Black question mark
ornament

Double exclamation
mark

Exclamation question
mark (or "interrobang")

Hundred points symbol
A+

Low brightness symbol

High brightness symbol

Trident emblem

Fleur-de-lis

Part alternation mark (start
of singer's part in traditional
Japanese music)

Warning sign

Children crossing

Japanese symbol for
beginner

Black universal recycling
symbol

Squared cjk unified
ideograph 6307
Finger or toe pointing

Chart with upwards
trend and yen sign

Sparkle

Eight-spoked asterisk

Negative squared
cross mark

White heavy checkmark

Diamond shape with a
dot inside

Cyclone

Double curly loop
Voice mail

Globe with meridians

Circled latin capital
letter M
Subway (metro)

89

Automated teller machine

Squared katakana sa *Service charge*

Passport control

Customs

Baggage claim

Left luggage

Wheelchair symbol

No smoking symbol

Water closet

Negative squared latin capital letter P *Parking*

Potable water symbol

Men's symbol

Women's symbol

Baby symbol

Restroom

Put litter in its place symbol

Cinema

Antenna with bars

Squared katakana koko
Destination or *here*

Squared NG
No good

Squared OK

Squared UP with exclamation mark
Level up (as in computer games)

Squared COOL

Squared NEW

Squared FREE

Numbers 0-10 in boxes

Input symbol for numbers

Black right-pointing
triangle
Play

Double vertical bar
Pause

Black right-pointing triangle
with double vertical bar
Play/pause

Black square for stop

Black circle for record

Black right-pointing
double triangle with
vertical bar
Skip to next chapter

Black left-pointing
double triangle with
vertical bar
Skip to previous chapter

Black right-pointing
double triangle
Fast forward

Black left-pointing
double triangle
Rewind

Twisted rightwards
arrows
Shuffle

Clockwise rightwards and
leftwards open circle arrows
Repeat

Clockwise open circle
arrows with circled one
Repeat track

Arrow
(multiple variations
exist)

Anticlockwise downwards
and upwards open circle
arrows
Refresh/reload

Rightwards arrow
with hook
Redo

ALL THE ARROWS

The symbols palette has many different
arrows for all manner of directions. We've
included one to give you an idea of what
they look like, but there's a little pointy sign
for any direction you'd care to go in. There's
even a double-headed arrow, to indicate a
straight line.

The "Black right-pointing triangle" (or "play")
and the "Black right-pointing double triangle"
("fast forward") symbols also have variations
pointing left, right, up, and down.

Leftwards arrow
with hook
Undo

Keycap number sign
Hashtag

Keycap asterisk

Information source

Input symbol for latin letters

Input symbol for symbols

Musical note

Multiple musical notes

Wavy dash
(used in some Asian scripts as a hyphen)

Curly loop

Heavy check mark

Clockwise downwards and upwards open circle arrows

Heavy plus sign

Heavy minus sign

Heavy division sign

Heavy multiplication X

Heavy dollar sign

Currency exchange

Copyright sign

Registered sign

Trademark sign

END with leftwards arrow above

BACK with leftwards arrow above

ON with exclamation mark with left right arrow above

TOP with upwards arrow above

SOON with rightwards arrow above

Ballot box with check

Radio button

Speaker

Speaker with one sound wave

Speaker with sound waves

Speaker with cancellation stroke
Mute

Cheering megaphone

Public address loudspeaker

OUT OF SHAPE

The symbols palette contains plenty of shapes – circles, squares, diamonds, triangles – that probably don't need defining, so we haven't included them here. But if you're feeling geometrically inclined or have an interest in creating your own Tetris screenshot with emoji, you'll find them on your device.

Bell
Alarm

Bell with cancellation stroke
Alarm off

Playing card black joker

Mahjong tile red dragon

Black spade suit

Black club suit

Black heart suit

Black diamond suit

Flower playing cards

Eye in speech bubble

WITNESS!

The "Eye in speech bubble" emoji is often used on social media as an instruction to look at something, or to hint at the mind's eye. Its actual origin is as an anti-bullying symbol. It combines an eye and speech bubble to encourage people who see bullying to speak out, as part of a campaign called "I am a witness", which is also another name for the symbol.

Thought balloon

Right anger bubble

Speech balloon

Clock face one o'clock
(multiple variations
available)

FLAGS

The flags included in the emoji keyboard come from an internationally-recognized set of country codes. Some countries don't have their own unique codes (such as Scotland and Wales, which are classified under the same code as Great Britain) so they do not have individual emoji flags.

| Afghanistan | Åland Islands | Albania | Algeria | American Samoa | Andorra |

| Angola | Anguilla | Antarctica | Antigua & Barbuda | Argentina | Armenia |

| Aruba | Australia | Austria | Azerbaijan | Bahamas | Bahrain |

| Bangladesh | Barbados | Belarus | Belgium | Belize | Benin |

| Bermuda | Bhutan | Bolivia | Bonaire, Sint Eustatius & Saba | Bosnia & Herzegovina | Botswana |

| Brazil | British Indian Ocean Territory | British Virgin Islands | Brunei | Bulgaria | Burkina Faso |

| Burundi | Cabo Verde | Cambodia | Cameroon | Canada | Canary Islands |

| Cayman Islands | Central African Republic | Chad | Chile | China | Christmas Island |

| Cocos (Keeling) Islands | Colombia | Comoros | Congo (Republic of the) | Congo (Democratic Republic of the) | Cook Islands |

| Costa Rica | Croatia | Cuba | Curaçao | Cyprus | Czech Republic |

| Denmark | Djibouti | Dominica | Dominican Republic | Ecuador | Egypt |

| El Salvador | Equatorial Guinea | Eritrea | Estonia | Ethiopia | European Union |

| Falkland Islands | Faroe Islands | Fiji | Finland | France | French Guiana |

| French Polynesia | French Southern Territories | Gabon | Gambia | Georgia | Germany |

| Ghana | Gibraltar | Greece | Greenland | Grenada | Guadeloupe |

| Guam | Guatemala | Guernsey | Guinea | Guinea-Bissau | Guyana |

| Haiti | Honduras | Hong Kong SAR China | Hungary | Iceland | India |

| Indonesia | Islamic Republic of Iran | Iraq | Ireland | Isle of Man | Israel |

| Italy | Ivory Coast (Côte d'Ivoire) | Jamaica | Japan | Jersey | Jordan |

FLAGS

Kazakhstan

Kenya

Kiribati

Kosovo

Kuwait

Kyrgyzstan

Laos

Latvia

Lebanon

Lesotho

Liberia

Libya

Liechtenstein

Lithuania

Luxembourg

Macau SAR China

Macedonia

Madagascar

Malawi

Malaysia

Maldives

Mali

Malta

Marshall Islands

Martinique

 Mauritania

 Mauritius

 Mayotte

 Mexico

 Micronesia

 Republic of Moldova

 Monaco

 Mongolia

 Montenegro

 Montserrat

 Morocco

 Mozambique

 Myanmar

 Namibia

 Nauru

 Nepal

 Netherlands

 New Caledonia

 New Zealand

 Nicaragua

 Niger

 Nigeria

 Niue

| Norfolk Island | North Korea | Northern Mariana Islands | Norway | Oman | Pakistan |

| Palau | Palestinian territories | Panama | Papua New Guinea | Paraguay | Peru |

| Philippines | Pitcairn | Poland | Portugal | Puerto Rico | Qatar |

| Réunion | Romania | Russian Federation | Rwanda | Saint Barthélemy | Saint Helena, Ascension & Tristan da Cunha |

Saint Kitts
& Nevis

Saint Lucia

Saint Pierre
& Miquelon

Saint Vincent &
the Grenadines

Samoa

San Marino

Sao Tome
& Principe

Saudi Arabia

Senegal

Serbia

Seychelles

Sierra Leone

Singapore

Sint Maarten
(Dutch part)

Slovakia

Slovenia

Solomon
Islands

Somalia

South Africa

South Georgia
& the South
Sandwich
Islands

South Korea

South Sudan

Spain

Sri Lanka

Sudan	Suriname	Swaziland	Sweden	Switzerland	Syrian Arab Republic

Taiwan	Tajikistan	United Republic of Tanzania	Thailand	Timor-Leste	Togo

Tokelau	Tonga	Trinidad & Tobago	Tunisia	Turkey	Turkmenistan

Turks & Caicos Islands	Tuvalu	Uganda	Ukraine	United Arab Emirates	United Kingdom

United States
of America

U.S. Virgin
Islands

Uruguay

Uzbekistan

Vanuatu

Vatican City

Venezuela

Vietnam

Wallis & Futuna

Western
Sahara

Yemen

Zambia

Zimbabwe

EMOJI ART

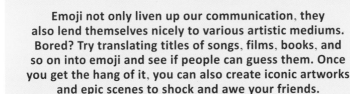

There's ongoing discussion about whether or not emoji can be considered a language of their own. With their wide range of symbols and icons to express everything from faith to feelings, are they a kind of twenty-first century pop art hieroglyphics?

Emoji not only liven up our communication, they also lend themselves nicely to various artistic mediums. Bored? Try translating titles of songs, films, books, and so on into emoji and see if people can guess them. Once you get the hang of it, you can also create iconic artworks and epic scenes to shock and awe your friends.

USEFUL PHRASES

This person wants to know where the bathroom is.

This person wants to know the price of something.

This person wants directions to the beach, on foot.

This person would like the chicken, please.

This person is in the mood for champagne.

This person doesn't feel so good and needs headache medicine.

This person wonders how you are.

A quick hello or goodbye from this person. (Beware! The static hand is offensive in some cultures, so keep it moving.)

This person wants to know if it's going to rain later.

This person is a vegetarian.

BOOKS

War and Peace

The Hunger Games

THERE SHE BLOWS!

Perhaps the most intriguing and ambitious emoji-related project to take place in the last few years is data engineer Fred Benenson's translation of *Moby Dick* (Herman Melville, 1851) into emoji. It was funded by Kickstarter and produced using Amazon Mechanical Turks, a system where people are paid to carry out small online tasks — three people translated each sentence, then the best one was voted on by others.

Is *Emoji Dick* a serious piece of cultural commentary or an astounding waste of time? It's up to you to decide, but the U.S. Library of Congress holds a copy, noting that it's an item that captures the zeitgeist of our fleeting digital age. We can ponder over it long after emoji have gone the way of the wax writing tablet.

Lord of the Rings

The Grapes of Wrath

LES MISERABLES

MOVIES

Back to the Future

Ghostbusters

Groundhog Day

Star Wars: The Force Awakens

AN EMOJI MOVIE!?

Rumours abound that emoji will soon be taking over a whole new medium. In the wake of the tremendous success of *The Lego Movie*, Sony Pictures Animation bought the rights to turn these beloved characters into film stars. No word yet on the plot or even which smileys and other creatures will make the cast, but we will all have our "Popcorn" at the ready!

Harry Potter and the Goblet of Fire

PLANET OF THE APES (1968)

EMOJI FUN

Setting words aside can be liberating for emoji! They can also be used to create or replicate works of art, movie posters, games, scenes from your imagination, and much, much more!

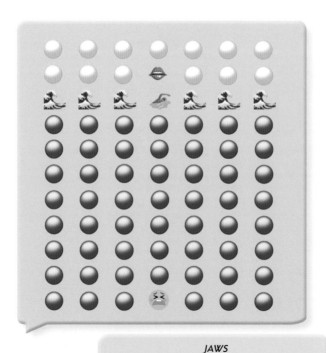

JAWS

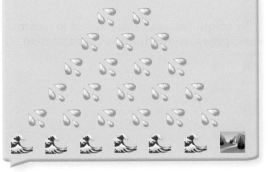

CRY ME A RIVER

LOVE!

CHECKERS?

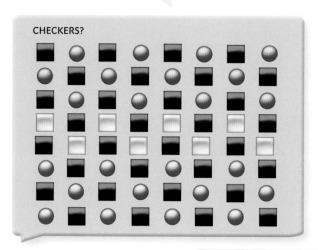

I'M MORE OF A CHESS MAN, MYSELF...

Perhaps emoji's greatest advantage over type is its capacity for whimsy. The world of emoji is one of pure imagination, so have fun and get carried away with it!

INDEX OF EMOJI

INDEX OF EMOJI

INDEX OF EMOJI

INDEX OF EMOJI